CONTENTS

Is there only one big ocean?

It seems that way. All the oceans flow into each other, but we know them as four different oceans – the Pacific, Atlantic, Indian and Arctic. The land we live on, the continents, rises out of the oceans. More than two-thirds of the Earth's rocky surface is covered by oceans.

Key
1. Arctic Ocean
2. Atlantic Ocean
3. Pacific Ocean
4. Indian Ocean
5. Southern Ocean

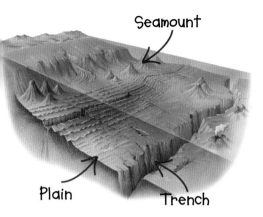

Seamount

Plain

Trench

Are there mountains under the sea?

Yes there are. The land beneath the sea is covered by mountains, flat areas called plains and deep valleys called trenches. There are also huge underwater volcanoes called seamounts.

Salty or fresh!

Almost all of the world's water is in the oceans. Only a tiny amount is in freshwater lakes and rivers.

Were do islands come from?

Islands are 'born' beneath the sea. If an underwater volcano erupts, it throws out hot, sticky lava. This cools and hardens in the water. Layers of lava build up and up, until a new island peeps above the waves.

Look

Look at the world map to find where you live. Which ocean is nearest to you?

Do seashells have feet?

Tiny animals called limpets live inside some seashells. They stick to rocks at the shoreline where they eat slimy, green plants called algae. When the tide is out, limpets stick to the rocks like glue, with a strong muscular foot. They only move when the tide crashes in.

Can starfish grow arms?

Yes they can. Starfish may have as many as 40 arms, called rays. If a hungry crab grabs hold of one, the starfish abandons its arm, and uses the others to make its getaway. It then begins to grow a new arm.

Limpets

Anemone

Starfish

4

Fighting fit!

Anemones are a kind of sea-living plant. Some anemones fight over their feeding grounds. Beadlet anemones shoot sharp, tiny hooks at each other until the weakest one gives in.

When is a sponge like an animal?

Sponges are animals! They are very simple creatures that filter food from sea water. The natural sponge that you use in the bath is a long-dead dried-out sponge!

Crab

Sponge

Find

When you next visit a beach, try to find a rockpool. Write a list of what you see.

Are there schools in the sea?

Some fish live in big groups called schools. This may protect them from hungry hunters. There are thousands of different types of fish in the sea. Most are covered in shiny scales and use fins and tails to swim. Fish have gills that take in oxygen from the water so that they can breathe.

Read

What is a big group of fish called? Read this page to find out.

6

Which fish looks like an oar?

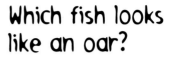

The oarfish does – and it can grow to be as long as four canoes! It is the longest bony fish and is found in all the world's oceans. Oarfish have a bright red fin along the length of their back. They swim upright through the water.

Oarfish

Flying high!

Flying fish cannot really fly. Fish can't survive out of water, but flying fish sometimes leap above the waves when they are swimming at high speed. They use their long fins to glide through the air for as long as 30 seconds.

Do fish like to sunbathe?

Sunfish like sunbathing. Ocean sunfish are huge fish that can weigh as much as one tonne – as heavy as a small car! They like to swim at the surface of the water, as if they're sunbathing.

School of fish

What is the scariest shark?

Great whites are the scariest sharks.
These huge fish speed through the water at 30 kilometres an hour. Unlike most fish, the great white shark has warm blood. This allows its muscles to work well but it also means that it needs to eat lots of meat. Great white sharks are fierce hunters. They will attack and eat almost anything, but prefer to feed on seals.

Great white shark

Draw

Using felt-tip pens, draw your own underwater picture. Include a great white shark.

Do some sharks use hammers?

Not really! Hammerhead sharks have hammer-shaped heads to search for food. With a nostril and an eye on each end of the 'hammer', they swing their heads from side to side, looking for a meal.

Hammerhead shark

Yum yum!

Most sharks are meat eaters. Herring are a favourite food for sand tiger and thresher sharks, while a hungry tiger shark will gobble up just about anything!

When is a shark like a pup?

When it's a baby. Young sharks are called pups. Some grow inside their mother's body. Others hatch from eggs straight into the sea.

Who builds walls beneath the sea?

Tiny animals build underwater walls.
These walls are made of coral,
the leftover skeletons of tiny sea
animals called polyps. Over millions
of years, enough skeletons pile up to
form walls. These make a coral reef.
All kinds of creatures live around a reef.

Parrot fish

Seahorse

Look

Do you know
where the Great
Barrier Reef is?
Look in an atlas
to find out.

Clownfish

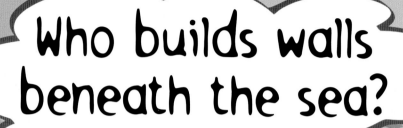

10

How do fish keep clean?

Cleaner wrasse are little fish that help other fish to keep clean! Larger fish, such as groupers and moray eels, visit the cleaner wrasse, which nibbles all the bugs and bits of dirt off the bigger fishes' bodies – what a feast!

Coral reef

Super reef

You can see the Great Barrier Reef from space! At over 2000 kilometres long, it is the largest thing ever built by living creatures.

Lionfish

Cleaner wrasse fish

When is a fish like a clown?

When it's a clownfish. These fish are brightly coloured, like circus clowns. They live among the stinging arms (tentacles) of the sea anemone. Clownfish swim among the stingers, where they are safe from enemies. The anemone doesn't seem to sting the clownfish.

Sea anemone

Why are whales so big?

Whales have grown to such a huge size because they live in water. The water helps to support their enormous bulk. The blue whale is the biggest animal in the ocean — and the whole planet. It is about 30 metres long and can weigh up to 150 tonnes. Every day, it eats about 4 tonnes of tiny, shrimp-like creatures called krill!

Blue whale

Can whales sing songs?

All whales make sounds, such as squeaks and moans. The humpback whale really does seem to sing. The males probably do this to attract a mate. He may repeat his song for up to 20 hours!

Humpback whale

Stick around!

Barnacles are shellfish. They attach themselves to ships, or the bodies of grey whales and other large sea animals.

Measure

The blue whale is 30 metres long. Can you measure how long you are?

Do whales grow tusks?

The narwhal has a tusk like a unicorn's. This tusk is a long, twirly tooth that comes out of the whale's head. The males use their tusks as weapons when they fight over females. The tusk can grow to 3 metres in length.

Are there crocodiles in the sea?

Most crocodiles live in rivers and swamps. The saltwater crocodile also swims out to sea – it doesn't seem to mind the salty water. These crocodiles are huge, and can grow to be 7 metres long and one tonne in weight.

Saltwater crocodile

Find out

Turtles only come ashore for one reason. Can you find out why?

Which lizard loves to swim?

Most lizards live on land, where it is easier to warm up their cold-blooded bodies. Marine iguanas depend on the sea for food. They dive underwater to eat seaweed growing on rocks. When they are not diving, they sit on rocks and soak up the sunshine.

How deep can a turtle dive?

Leatherback turtles can dive up to 1200 metres for their dinner. They are the biggest sea turtles and they make the deepest dives. Leatherbacks feed mostly on jellyfish but also eat crabs, lobsters and starfish.

Leatherback turtle

Slithery snakes!

There are poisonous snakes in the sea. The banded sea snake and the yellow-bellied sea snake both use poison to kill their prey. Their poison is far stronger than that of land snakes.

15

Can seabirds sleep as they fly?

Wandering albatrosses are the biggest seabirds and spend months at sea. They are such good gliders that they even sleep as they fly. To feed, they sit on the surface of the water, where they catch creatures such as squid. An albatross has a wingspan of around 3 metres — about the length of a family car!

Wandering albatross

Think

Sea birds have webbed feet. Why do you think this is? Do you have webbed feet?

Do seabirds dig burrows?

Most seabirds make nests on cliffs. The puffin digs a burrow on the clifftop, like a rabbit. Sometimes, a puffin even takes over an empty rabbit hole. Here it lays its egg. Both parents look after the chick when it hatches.

Puffins

Dancing birds!

Boobies are a type of seabird that live in large groups. The males have bright red or blue feet. When they are looking for a mate, they dance in front of the female, trying to attract her with their colourful feet!

Which bird dives for its dinner?

The gannet dives headfirst into the ocean to catch fish in its beak. It dives at high-speed and hits the water hard. Luckily, the gannet is protected by cushions of air inside its head that absorb most of the shock.

How do polar bears learn to swim?

Polar bears are good swimmers and they live around the freezing Arctic Ocean. They learn to swim when they are cubs, by following their mother into the water. With their big front paws, the bears paddle through the water. They can swim for many hours.

Polar bears

Imagine
Pretend to be a penguin. Imagine what life is like at the South Pole.

Are penguins fast swimmers?

Penguins are birds – but they cannot fly. All penguins are fast swimmers. The fastest swimmer is the gentoo penguin. It can reach speeds of 27 kilometres an hour underwater.

Gentoo penguin

Small and tall!

The smallest penguin is the fairy penguin at just 40 centimetres tall. The biggest is the emperor penguin at 1.3 metres in height – as tall as a seven-year-old child!

Which penguin dad likes to babysit?

Emperor penguin dads look after the baby chicks. The female lays an egg and leaves her mate to keep it warm. The penguin dad balances the egg on his feet to keep it off the freezing ice. He goes without food until the chick hatches. When it does, the mother returns and both parents look after it.

Is seaweed good to eat?

Seaweed can be very good to eat. In shallow, warm seawater, people can grow their own seaweed. It is then dried in the sun, which helps to keep it fresh. Seaweed is even used to make ice cream!

Growing seaweed

List

Make a list of the things you can eat that come from the ocean. Which of these things have you eaten before?

How do we get salt from the sea?

Sea water is salty. Salt is an important substance. In hot, low-lying areas, people build walls to hold shallow pools of sea water. The water dries up in the sun, leaving behind crystals of salt.

How are lobsters caught?

Lobsters are large shellfish that are good to eat. Fishermen catch them in wooden cages called pots. The lobsters are attracted to dead fish placed in the pots. They push the door of the pot open to get to the fish, but once inside, the lobster can't get out again.

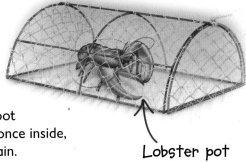

Lobster pot

Do pearls grow at sea?

Yes they do. Pearls grow inside oysters, a kind of shellfish. If a grain of sand gets stuck in an oyster's shell, it irritates its soft body. The oyster coats the grain with a substance that it uses to line the inside of its shell. In time, more coats are added and a pearl begins to form.

21

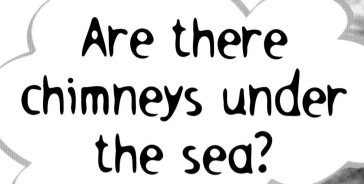

Are there chimneys under the sea?

Rocky chimneys on the ocean floor give off clouds of hot water. These chimneys lie deep beneath the ocean. The hot water feeds strange creatures such as tube worms and sea spiders.

Rat tail fish

Watery village!

In 1963, diver Jacques Cousteau built a village on the bed of the Red Sea. Along with four other divers, he lived there for a whole month.

Giant clams

Do monsters live in the sea?

Sea monsters do not exist. Long ago, people thought they did. The giant squid may have been mistaken for a monster. It has long arms called tentacles, and eyes as big as dinner plates.

← Giant squid

What is a mermaid?

Mermaids are strange creatures with the body of a woman and a long fishy tail – but they aren't real. People once thought they lived in the sea and confused sailors with their beautiful singing.

Chimney

Sea spider

Tube worms

Write

Can you think of any stories or films about mermaids? See if you can write your own underwater mermaid story.

Index

First published in 2006 by
Miles Kelly Publishing Ltd,
Harding's Barn, Bardfield End Green,
Thaxted, Essex, CM6 3PX, UK

Copyright © Miles Kelly Publishing Ltd 2006

This edition published 2012

2 4 6 8 10 9 7 5 3 1

Publishing Director Belinda Gallagher
Creative Director Jo Cowan
Volume Designer Michelle Cannatella
Cover Designer Jo Cowan
Indexer Susan Bosanko
Production Manager Elizabeth Collins
Reprographics Stephan Davis, Lorraine King
Character Cartoonist Mike Foster

ISBN 978-1-84810-899-8

Printed in China

British Library Cataloguing-in-Publication Data
A catalogue record for this book is available from the British Library

ACKNOWLEDGEMENTS
All artwork from the Miles Kelly Artwork Bank
The publishers would like to thank Shutterstock for the use of the cover photograph
All other photographs are from:
Corel, digitalSTOCK, digitalvision, John Foxx, PhotoAlto, PhotoDisc, PhotoEssentials, PhotoPro, Stockbyte
Every effort has been made to acknowledge the source and copyright holder of each picture. Miles Kelly Publishing apologises for any unintentional errors or omissions.

Made with paper from a sustainable forest

www.mileskelly.net
info@mileskelly.net

www.factsforprojects.com

24